After the Tour

POETRY

Jennifer Minniti-Shippey

CALYPSO EDITIONS

CALYPSO EDITIONS
www.CalypsoEditions.org

Copyright 2018 by Jennifer Minniti-Shippey
© 2018 Calypso Editions
All rights reserved

Author photography: James Forsyth

Book Layout & Cover Design: Katie Stapko
www.stapkodesign.com

ISBN 13: 978-1-944593-07-0

No part of this book may be reproduced by any means without permission of the publisher.

First edition, November 2018
Printed in the United States

After the Tour

Contents

FOR THE TOWER
For the Tower	3

AFTER THE TOUR
To the boy reading *Harry Potter* on his bunk in Afghanistan	9
Elegy I	11
Second Tour	12
Third Tour	14
Counting Wild Horses	15
For Jerry	17
Alexander Pelham, 1992 – 2014	19
Rachel Dean, 1981 – 2006	20
America	21
Grief	23
After news of a high school friend's death,	24
Elegy II	27
The Prairie All Around Us	28
Last Days of June	29
Psalm	30

BOOK OF SEDUCTIONS

Deployment	33
Ecclesiastes of the Denver Strip Club	34
September (1)	36
The Pamphlet Man	37
Jane's Letter of Recommendation	38
Each morning at eight, the phone rings	39
September (2)	40
February	41
Gifts for the cruelest month	44
Neal, loving you	46
Let it be during an earthquake.	49
The Seductions of Isabelle Jackson	50
Moonlighting as the Angel of Death	63

IN THE LAND OF LINNEA

When my dead meet they hold hands	67
Notes	70
Acknowledgments	71

FOR THE TOWER

FOR THE TOWER

For the tower may have sweet cows
bundled in black & white around its base,
green moss may creep
along its cool southern stones.
For you may stand top the tower crushing
lavender in your palm, cast for other towers
and find none as high as this.

For in this tower, you could raise a waddling,
warbling son, teach him to race up
the winding stair,
to shoot from arrow slits
pebbles at Jehovah's Witnesses, stray dogs.

You make names for the tower:
swale of grass where the moat lies buried
you'll name Alfred, you'll pace top the tower
crushing lavender shouting *Yeats!*
Ballycoole! Tourmaline!
until the air exudes your breath.

For the tower's climbing rose vines in white,
pink. For cherry trees marching

to the horizon of hills. The possibility
of potatoes underground.
The tower requires a cat
to mouse, requires a larder,
root cellar, guards.

For you've been trying to build this tower
in the backyard of your rented apartment for years.
You planted lavender, crushed it.
You shouted out, shouted,
and the air echoed,
and the upstairs Rottweiler nearly lunged out the window.

The tower stinks of freedom, still water.
For the tower, you would turn stones
centuries fallow, walk long miles
behind a mule and in the plowed lines
plant mustard seed.

Oh, may there be yellow corn
in the fields of the tower,
cows and potatoes, clear days,

may the tower make a fool out of you,
may you speak to the tower
other names for the heart:
fortress, citadel, stronghold, fastness.

TO THE BOY READING *HARRY POTTER* ON HIS BUNK IN AFGHANISTAN

You are at twenty a man:
you fight with bullets.
It's too bright-hot to read.

The monotony of waiting bent only
by more waiting,
and your lieutenant mutters

oh god, please,
someone shoot at us today.
Three weeks with no fire—

the book's spine broken so when open,
it lies flat on your chest
like shrunken,

misplaced wings. Your brothers play
card games out of bright-hot boredom.
Some you love return—you'll greet them

with a fist to solar plexus, generous
sweep of boot to shin. Blood out,
blood in. It's a kind of wisdom.

Three weeks, no fire. You're lying on your bunk,
boots on, tracing the spine
of *Harry Potter*. Next to you,

rifle rests on dark-green blanket,
like it dreams of rivers,
red-haired women.

Like it will wake in the early morning,
twist with thirst, desire. Like when asked,
how many bullets were there,

it might answer, *as many
as there were stars in the sky.*
Three weeks, no fire.

ELEGY I

The only maps I know are for bodies,
skin and relenting flesh, the compass rose
pointing north, north between the scapula
of my lover. Ink fades, borders hunger
to be crossed. To map my lover's spine:
it must be north. Soft sweet skin,
north. Skin and relentless flesh.

SECOND TOUR

While we are still young one morning and the sun
peeks into the house like a boy
under a circus tent to the applauding rain

that falls somewhere in west Kentucky,
I hope the aspens flutter in a breeze
so quick you could race it

and that the loneliness we will one day
know falls also in west Kentucky—
in this minute or ten before breakfast—

and that we kiss
pushed against the wall not fighting
age so much as waiting

for its possible grace, and I hope we kiss
like it means our survival, not knowing
need from god or skeletons of mammoths,

those ancients carved out
of the badlands and displayed
like proof of magic to wide-eyed children—

I hope while we shove ourselves together in the hallway half-dressed and kissing, we feel the scale of the earth beneath us, its ballast, its weight.

THIRD TOUR

there's waiting, then *wait* and
how dare you take so long to get here,

air blasted past dust and dusty blinds,
detonation of overripe, out-seasoned

vine-grown tomatoes, so
come through, blown open:

I'll make tea, pay half the bills,
we'll census dead birds and marvel

at their eyes still, still
unblinking into us

COUNTING WILD HORSES

The most efficient way
to count
wild horses
is helicopter flights—the great
speed and whir
of blades in air drives
mustangs from the brush

We count them
three piebald
seven chestnut
two roan
all grey with dust of the plain

Over the low thrum
of the heli comes
the rumble
of hooves black
cracked from shifting rocks
and shale

They gallop towards the ravine
below them, the river

Just when it seems
we will lose them all
they peel from the brink

manes swirling
like plover wings
over salt-damp sand

FOR JERRY

The whole thing isn't much: a man
from Oregon, on the border of boyhood in 1968,

fled. He crossed from Washington
to Canada,

or tried—the guards, who looked busy,
stopped him. He didn't want to fight,

and he didn't fight.
They stopped him and put him in the army.

It was a good army, he said later.
I thought, though, they trained you better.

He thought they trained you.
They airlifted him into Khe Sanh on a Friday,

then they fought.
No-one brought more bullets.

He was so careful,
strangers died before they knew he was there.

*

It's a small country. His officer couldn't remember
the man's grey-green, green-black fatigues.

On Monday, a platoon found him
squatting in his mud-wrecked hole.

Why didn't you come back?
The man shrugged his shoulders.

The shrug said he'd made a good soldier.
It said he'd learned to shoot.

The question seemed reasonable.
The man wouldn't be fooled.

The man had a strong arm.
He believed he'd known something right.

Take careful aim. Don't speak.
And in the army, in Khe Sanh especially,
it was a simple thing to know.

ALEXANDER PELHAM, 1992 — 2014

Your ass in that chair,
there on the patio in the dark of a Wednesday,
bark of the bougainvillea eaten silent by loopers,
neighbor dogs bark, you're reading a Dylan Thomas poem
not quite by memory, the calm
belovéd monologue: I gave you Elizabeth Bishop. I'd practiced
in the shower, her words some kind of Babel-tower of hope—

I didn't know losing you would be like Bishop
claimed—you remember, you recorded:
                                    she said it was an easy
thing to master, and that empty chair is vaster than the patio,
lit by the lights you bought me, the gift
you made faster than I could thank you, and how
will I thank you now,

your ass as far gone as Thomas, not gently:
stop quoting poems at me, stop,
laughter, stop Wednesdays,
and go ahead, brave loopers,
chewing on the dark.

RACHEL DEAN, 1981 – 2006

Neglected by all things
                                    save summer and fighter jets

we stretched on sand

                and in you quiet brewed the war
*

summer: a mockery of mountains
                sweat in couch covers
summer was a body within your body
brown horses with long manes
summer made legs and a heartbeat
made eavesdropping lonelier
summer: skin out of cells
summer made pain, pain

*

Summer—and fighter jets, summer and fighter jets.

Good bye daughter

              fighter jets, neglect us

AMERICA

of steel-toed boots and fixed-gear bicycles,
O country of subwoofers and subterranean shelters,

of men on green fields in armor, of men on sand
in skin, of skin on skin, and nail polish named
better than our children—

let me spell out
short, declarative sentences: the marigolds
still bloom in the planter boxes. Mourning doves

bead phone lines like dew. Mourning girls
braid yellow ribbons into their black hair.
I am trivializing music with grief.

Let me make this accessible:
my brother died in the tar sands. My brother
died in a coal pit in West Virginia. My

brother died in Afghanistan.
Small caliber breath breaches
beneath bullets, beneath—I

don't have a brother, but I have yellow ribbons
for every lost man. O ripe avocados.
O beards on the chins of beautiful men.

GRIEF

        comes
uninvited

        (Listen now
hear
        fire in the eucalyptus
            one
ravaged, white scarred wrist)

& yet

        somehow radiant

AFTER NEWS OF A HIGH SCHOOL FRIEND'S DEATH,

we lace our tennis shoes. To the dog's collar,
clip a gold-and-green leash—colors of Eugene,
Duck fight song we learned at ten by rote.
Purple trees crackle with crow feathers.

We are not old enough to die in reasonable ways.
David's cycling accident, hit
at 13th and Willamette,
roll calls the already dead:

our friend Skye, shot
in his apartment at twenty-two, and our friend
Lucas, who killed him. A car
backfires, Skye.

Walking down Ash Street,
we squint to read again the gun
and the story, Lucas, of loss.
There was a girl. A girl,

and two boys on the blade of manhood.
A door opening, days of dark years
and Prozac, police lights.
Police lights where you lay dying, David.

A stoplight not quite red. You stood
at John Henry's bar a year ago, bought
a shot of whiskey, sported a leather jacket. Did
we speak? The walk doesn't answer.

We walk. The walk is a prayer.
A pilgrim, the dog. Beneath our black Converse
the sidewalk is the Willamette River,
a grass field, graves. A footbridge

crossing Amazon Parkway, west towards
South Eugene High. There's a gladness
in everything still breathing.
Our sisters say the body of David Minor

arced thirty feet through air. They say
his bicycle was blue.
The walk is a prayer, but the walk
cannot turn the light red, the prayer

does not shut the door,
the opening door, cannot unfire the gun.
Stay where you are in our first mind,
commands the walk.

Skye, stay, be the kind of guy our fathers
approve of—teach us to cook fresh pasta,
tango. Lose your virginity
to our best friend after junior prom in Sadie's basement.

We walk after hearing of another friend's death,
we clip the Duck leash to the dog, towards our first
mind we walk, back to our first mind.
We say the names. Those purple trees are jacaranda.

We say, those purple trees are jacaranda.

ELEGY II

Bless the bullet as it leaves the gun.
Bless the brain, the heart.
After, bless the silence and all the things named:

bless the tongue with seven stitches,
the bruised cheekbone, cracked teeth.
Bless his brown eye, grey coat,

blind spot, tumor,
the nerve unraveling, bless.
Bless the young bodies that do not rise,

bless them black, bless them grey,
bless the grace of a body in flight.
Bless the silence.

THE PRAIRIE ALL AROUND US

Where are you, Isabelle Jackson?
Above the blue-green grasslands, buzzards make spirals
in the blue, the heat is, just *is*, shimmering in the nowhere—

Calling for you, Isabelle, and the coyotes pause
their patient stalking. Pause, frozen breath, fat mice beneath
the green-dark grass. Pause the kearing whistle of red-tailed hawk.

The sun makes a prison of the prairie: beetles prisoners,
black-banded snakes, lost bison tangled in gold chains of light.
A western shore of grass. The mountain blacked with cloud.

Strands of barbed wire jeweled with seed, downy feathers,
blood. Thin aspens in the creekbed rustle in the western
breeze, Isabelle, Isabelle, are you there?

Silence snaps down the backs of the coyotes,
silence, and the prairie all around us. The breeze.

LAST DAYS OF JUNE

A whole sun-skinned nation
later and I am on my knees
in the trolley, the trolley south
bound, everything dark and rattling—
June in this country comes
jacarandad and sky-bruised—and me
wailing hallelujah quite
silently, good-bye brave ponies
grazing in the green wind, good-
bye thin socks abandoned
to the soft mercies of rain,
good-bye plastic peonies on the high
heels of happiness.
I am trying, just try
ing to love this again, my life.

PSALM

The coyote
      haunts the creekbed
      trots in front of me. He flicks a red ear
but does not slow,

limp body
of a ground squirrel flowering from his mouth.

You are a country open to death,

      you, the horizon of barking dogs.

Snails crackle under my heel.

Brush back the branches and lift your wings of knives.

You are not consolation.

You are the dark sound.

BOOK OF SEDUCTIONS

DEPLOYMENT

Roger, before I forget—

I left my bikini
the blue one with white flowers
on the floor

of the room in Florida
and I hope you
brought it back

You couldn't miss it
crumpled
still wet

from our late swim
You untied
the strings

tangled
your fingers
in my hair

ECCLESIASTES OF THE DENVER STRIP CLUB

to everything there is a season
and a time for every purpose under neon lights

time for opening the doors of the old opera house
for a short bouncer and no cover charge

time for champagne and bubbles in the champagne
time for strapless bras time for citrus perfume for zippers

for pink pasties for sparkling tassels for heels
and painted toenails

time to introduce yourself to a blackhaired dancer
to give a fake name in exchange for hers

time to watch her boom box tattoo flex and stretch
as she bends pale skin over the stage

time to order a lap dance for your lesbian friend
to order a dance for yourself

time to light the cigarette of the blackhaired dancer
to call her sweetness perhaps perhaps to not

there is finally a time of Johnny Walker Blue and dizzied
by the flashing lights to wish for a cab

a time to leave east Denver
it is time gentlemen
it is time

SEPTEMBER (1)

You're a fantasy girl now, he says
about fifteen seconds before he kisses me, and I know
we're talking football, quarterback comps,
yards after contact, our fall vocabulary—
but this statement
is so exciting I rip the black spaghetti strap
of the soft black dress I wore to his studio braless
so he could rip it off me,
and stand for a moment
in the glow of my breasts and say words
to that effect

THE PAMPHLET MAN

He knocks
in a crisp white shirt
new tie
collecting
his soul for the week.

He and his black backpack.

Sometimes,
if she shuts the screen
in his face
he says "I'll pray
for you
if you
won't pray yourself."

One foot
resting atop the other,
she doesn't believe him.

Her and her shutters drawn.

JANE'S LETTER OF RECOMMENDATION

She taught your hair to fall in your eyes,
your mouth to lick mango salsa
from your fingertips in public, to say yes,
to say yes, yes.

You leave her fully dressed
in Asheville on a hotel bed,
walk out
under a stoplight blinking red.

She will wake with a letter
of recommendation to give her next great love.

Take her, it says,
but with a shield of salt.
She will be darker forever than you
and more desirable.

EACH MORNING AT EIGHT, THE PHONE RINGS

You must imagine me
as I was then,
but my hair is longer now.

(The phone rings, rings.
Roger, I say to the ringing.)

No, it was *you*
who said, I'd marry you
if you drank less whiskey.
I drink, remember, gin.

When you see me again,
it'll be summer.
I'll wear black
aviator sunglasses, and a green dress.
Please bring the bikini
I left on top of your dryer.

Roger, I say to the ringing,
my hair is longer now.

SEPTEMBER (2)

Love is a leash, I declare at two a.m.
on a Thursday, we're deep in an internet search
for adoptable dogs—and I'm talking dogs not metaphors.
Even the best dog will chase a squirrel ghost or
rabbit into the road and leave you
anguished on the blistered asphalt (I believe
too in the metaphor, and imagine the skin motes
and sweat we string between our bodies binding
with every open-mouthed ah but this isn't love not love not

FEBRUARY

in the mountains east of San Diego
        riding a bay horse

Conrad   I think of you

                      I hold the reins loose in one fist

Half-bloom mountain lilac shudder
     in this sea wind

It's raining here   brother

raining at night politely

stray grass   blades up through red rocks

my bay horse crops it down

I balance on loneliness like on my horse

shoulders back, chest open

        grip with inner thigh   inner calf

        its breathing heart

heels down   I lower my gravity's center

    is there gravity

in white tails of rabbits

    they flee from our heavy hooves

        shiver under lilacs

black skeletons
    of the last fire

        haunt the trail

twist black fingers in   and   out
of white blooming vines

what names they have I don't know

Conrad I know   bay for horse

lilac   for purple cones
          long as thumb nail to wrist bone

grass exhausted, we wander on

stir dust under wet earth's film

It's sun   then clouds today

                 chasing from west and the sea

we're longing for the same
oh brother my bay horse and I

          green fields   Conrad   green fields

GIFTS FOR THE CRUELEST MONTH

Not owning a record player, I bought
Pink Floyd. I purchased
brown cowboy boots,
a black ballcap,
stole a pink paper-flower lei from a bar.

Three dinners for a friend
who looked as if she'd been living
on sunlight for years.

I gave myself every night at the Turf Club
for two weeks in the middle of the month,
four strangers, two friends,
one bartender pressing me against the beer cooler,
and then a blessedly empty bed.

My greying dog I took to the beach once—
the water still winter-cold, so we sat
in damp sand and I covered my toes
and her paws with sand.

I offered the month a day off,
on which I would cease to blame it, and maybe
we could watch a football game together.

April never wanted to be January—
I should have known better.

I notice now
that I am the only one giving gifts.

What more, I wonder,
could I accept.

NEAL, LOVING YOU

is like loving the man who boards an airplane
armed with a red plaid shirt
one cigarette and an undeclared
pack of matches

The FBI interrogates me for hours:

his blond eyelashes, did you kiss them

his cracked fingernails, did you kiss them

the dark hair on his chest,
    did you take it in your teeth

and Neal I will confess everything: Yes.

*

Yes to the space between your collarbones,
where I would subsidize corn fields,
wheat fields, buffalo

Yes to Thanksgiving in Virginia, football
on mute in the kitchen,
the shotguns warm in your brother's arms
and across your hip

*

You flirt with me, America—
wrap me in your arms
      three times a night
You pour another glass of champagne
teach me to sing *Buffalo Soldier* in a taxi

I love even your infidelities:
I kiss them on the lips.

*

Night: my hand
on your brown boot

Your fingers
trace the seam of my jeans

When I touch your skin, Neal, I touch

west Texas

Free Union, Virginia   Las Cruces
I long, over every inch of you, to rub my palms

*

You are silver snap buttons, stonemason
        of desire—

        Neal

when I look in your eyes I see

plains of our history

blue mountains on either side of this country

For the country in your eyes, I hunger

LET IT BE DURING AN EARTHQUAKE.

Let it be half a bottle of champagne, or three
gin & tonics later.

Be on a catamaran,
a sidewalk,
a brown gelding.

On a weathered deck, slapping mosquitoes.

Whenever it arrives, it arrives
with you beneath the white doorframe,
half-asleep, walls shuddering,

and you may have blue eyes or green, you may
be undressed already,

you slip across skin your trembling hands,
feel ribs and desire, only,

and then there is no earthquake, only three gin & tonics,
and later—
whenever it arrives,
it arrives.

THE SEDUCTIONS OF ISABELLE JACKSON

I, Isabelle Jackson, am done dating DJs

because he'd rather carry a case of new vinyl than flowers
through the door at three a.m.
and every time he touches my breasts
he's mixing hot new singles, my nipples as volume control

I'm done dating chefs because he refuses to wash his splotched white hat
as it's the locus of his cooking mojo
and when he hangs it on my bedpost
the air fills with lemon, rosemary, and grease fires,
and because with chefs,
spooning always leads to forking
and sometimes I just want to be held

Dating bartenders, I'm done,
because she has learned how to drink tequila without
wrinkling her nose while some guy stares down her shirt,
to toss an open beer bottle across the bar without spilling a drop,
and to look at everyone as if
she's seen them naked
I'm tired of wondering if she has

But I'm done dating writers
most of all
because he ices too much scotch
and believes all its superlatives:
he's got the most chiseled biceps,
sexiest belt buckle,
hippest fake-wood watch
in the room,
and of course, says the scotch,
he's the hero of all my poems

Laundry

Yellow daylilies strewn on the hardwood floor.
In the sunlit living room, one sandal.

One sandal in the kitchen, where a glass
of ice water beads.

Black cotton bra.
Puddle of blue shirt, discarded

jeans. The open bedroom door.
Two brown bodies tangled in white sheets.

Two Weeks In March

I. Izzi's Day Without a Drink

She strums her fingers on the bar top,
middle, ring, pinkie, thumb.

A beer.
A tall beer, she orders
a tall dark beer to swallow up the shake,
and it does.

It tastes like rainwater,
like dew in the desert, it tastes
like blood tastes to a drought-starved lion,

and she hums,
claws curled around the cup.

II. Email from Isabelle's Father

River otters have come to live in Coyote Creek
again this year! I saw four at six a.m.,
their paws muddy from the silt,
splashing. I tried to sneak
up, but they heard the damn dogs
coming and—like that!
The old fern bog
is dry, and I'm worried about the young
Doug fir we planted. Soon I'll take the plunge
and lug around that lime green watering can.
A great blue heron lifts up as I write,
and this morning I saw two harriers, and the black-shouldered
kite. Coffee on the porch, I could have sat out there
all month, but your mom said, Michael, come inside,
and you might laugh, but she's serious.
We remind me of black bears,
waking from oak to oak, our sweet growling.

III. Isabelle's Evening with Jane

Cocaine and celery, she says, black hair
falling across her eyes, *that's how you lose
ten pounds this week.* She cuts

another line with my driver's license.
Her small thumb covers my face,
halo of blonde hair framing her nail.

She leaves mirror on nightstand,
walks to the kitchen.
I hear the suck
of the fridge door opening,

and the heart, from its great distance, watches.

Isabelle is grateful

to her sister's right fallopian tube, which did not hold an embryo
for six weeks and
which did not burst
to fill her peritoneal cavity with blood—
did not evict the chief of surgery from his OR

the right fallopian tube
did not leave her
three scars in a band across her belly

did not fingerprint the doctor
blue on her navel's edge

the right fallopian tube remains
whole

she strokes her stomach
absently
and it is the right tube Isabelle thanks,
the warm flesh,
and pausing there,
her hand

I want to make environmentalism really good-looking

I want to slip off its Birkenstocks
and woolen socks,
pumice its soles.

I want to shave the legs of environmentalism.

Trade its long tie-dyed skirt
for a sexy and soulful
plaid mini. Substitute a red thong.

Environmentalism, under my care,
will wash its hair four times
a week, cut in bangs, use styling gel
and a blow dryer.

To environmentalism I give a pocket mirror.

Tenderly I will teach environmentalism
about waterproof mascara.

Since this green planet
cannot dress to impress—not Antarctica,
star-nosed moles, lichen, not saguaro cactus
nor coyotes,
environmentalism must

turn apathy into lust,
hike the old growth in black high heels
with cherry-red soles.

How to Train a Racehorse

From the pink lining
of his nostrils, rub dirt.
Tell him, in whispered
Spanish—a good language
for talking to horses—*oye,
caballo bueno. Amor. Suerte.*

Run your palms down
his tendons, curse
swollen ligaments.
Liniment, stall rest,
handwalks. Clench your hands
so scars white your knuckles.
Blame yourself, for breezing him
too fast. Blame the damn colt,
for already knowing to win,
for stretching his chocolate nose
out in front, pricking his ears
as he swept under the wire.

Watch him be walked
through the shedrow, how the sun
dapples his dark coat. Tug one satin ear
close, say again: listen, good horse.
Love. Luck. When you stroke
his neck, he will push his nose
into your flat palm,
blow hot steam.

Izzi Hates Feet

Slipping the leather sandal
off your foot,
dragging my fingers
across the sweat marks left by your toes:
for me, love must be so.

I must lie down opposite you,
lift your rough foot and place it on my chin.

Heel presses jawbone,
cheek fits in sole's arch.
Pads of toes rest on smooth temple,
ball of foot under half-closed eyes.

MOONLIGHTING AS THE ANGEL OF DEATH

I know this is a desirable
position, but I believe
I have qualities necessary
to make a great death.

I love to sleep in. If hired,
no-one will die in the morning.

I promise to honor as many last wishes
as possible.

I accept
no bribes. I cause
no pain, I

as death, will only come in the rain.

I will come with shower-wet hair, and cut-out
cardboard wings, and black serpents
tattooed around my wrists—
Their heads will swallow their tails,
so we remember we are made of earth,

and as earth we shall all return.

IN THE LAND OF LINNEA

WHEN MY DEAD MEET THEY HOLD HANDS

In the land of Linnea   and   of Sarah
red bougainvillea blossoms
      by whipping wind   are blown
through the heavy oak door.

The wind blows also through light-bodies.

      This one has eyes
          she speaks
              On the left, she has a voice
                  she watches

They crowd me.

Breasts press against my elbows
         warm palms in my back's hollow
    a tongue in the dark   of my mouth.
                                        .

A jade-green hummingbird in the red arbor,
                wings shiver wings in my hair

        they whisper

                as they lean   close above me

                                                as they stay.

                        Why

     are the straw hats in the middle of the highway?   I shout.

    Memory replaces nothing, not
            brown eyes or blue, not
                  blonde hair or

bones or skin.

to my dead, living
        to my dead, living jade-green
                to my living dead, jade-green

NOTES

"The Pamphlet Man" owes a debt to Rita Ann Higgins.

"For Jerry" owes a debt to Alberto Ríos.

"Second Tour" owes a debt to Steve Scafidi.

"Deployment" owes a debt to William Carlos Williams.

ACKNOWLEDGMENTS

This book was a long time in the making, and that leaves a long list of people and places and institutions to thank. Joyfully!

Many thanks to the editors of the following publications, in which some of the poems in this book first appeared: *Salamander, Cider Press Review, In Posse Review, Jackson Hole Review, San Diego Poetry Annual,* and *Pure Francis.*

Several of these poems appeared in *Done Dating DJs,* winner of the 2009 Fool for Poetry Chapbook Competition, sponsored by the Munster Literature Centre of Cork, Ireland. *Done Dating DJs* was published by Southword Editions. Thanks, Patrick Cotter, Leanne O'Sullivan, and the wonderful poets I met at the Éigse Festival.

Another several of these poems appeared in the chapbook *Earth's Horses & Boys,* from Finishing Line Press in March, 2013. Thanks to Christen Kincaid and Leah Maines, as well.

Thanks to Matthew Nevin, Ciara Scanlan, and the community at MART, Dublin, for welcoming me to a writing residency to work on these poems in the summer of 2016. And for the lunch performance that day in 2013, you remember, there was a table and a fire station and innocent bystanders.

Thanks to the teachers, classmates, and poets I've known at Randolph-Macon Woman's College & San Diego State University, who inspire me with their work, their passion, and their joy. An incomplete list: Sandra Alcosser, Hari Alluri, Garrett Bryant, Camille Dungy, Piotr Florcyzk, Amanda Fuller, Brian Hayter, Taylor Mardis Katz, David Tomas Martinez, Carly Joy Miller, Jim Peterson, Francine Rockey, Erin Rodini, Monica Zobel.

To my collaborators, instigators, champions, friends, with love: Katie Farris, Lyndsey Lederer, Mat Raney, Dean Robertson, Adam Veal, Emily Vizzo, Katriona Woods.

Thanks forever to Ilya Kaminsky, mentor, editor-in-chief, advocate, and friend.

Martin Woodside, who has read more of these poems than any person could reasonably expect, and who makes me a better writer every time: thank you.

Thank you, finally, to my wonderful, supportive family.

About the Publisher

Calypso Editions is a cooperative, artist-run, 501(c)(3) non-profit press dedicated to publishing quality literary books of poetry and fiction with a global perspective.

We believe that literature is essential to building an international community of readers and writers and that, in a world of digital saturation, books can serve as physical artifacts of beauty and wonder.

CALYPSO EDITIONS

info@CalypsoEditions.org | www.CalypsoEditions.org

More Original Poetry
Calypso Editions
www.CalypsoEditions.org

Houston's Favorite Poems
Edited by Robin Davidson
Poetry

Speak, My Tongue
by Carrie Meadows
Poetry

Blue Structure
by Jan Freeman
Poetry

While Everything Slipped Away From Me
by Erika Lutzner
Poetry

Contemporary Poetry in Translation
Calypso Editions
www.CalypsoEditions.org

Wild Geese Sorrow
New Translations by
Jeffrey Thomas Leong

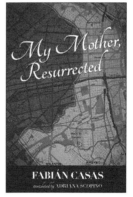

My Mother, Resurrected
by Fabián Casas
Translated by Adriana Scopino
Poetry

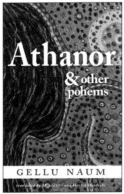

Athanor and Other Pohems
by Gellu Naum
Translated by Margento and
Martin Woodside
Poetry

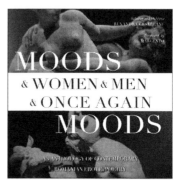

*Moods & Women & Men & Once Again
Moods: An Anthology of Contemporary
Romanian Erotic Poetry*
Edited by Ruxandra Cesereanu
Poetry

Original Fiction and Nonfiction
Calypso Editions
www.CalypsoEditions.org

The Little Trilogy
by Anton Chekhov
Translated by Boris Dralyuk
Fiction

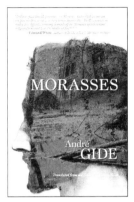

Morasses
by André Gide
Translated by Tadzio Koelb
Fiction

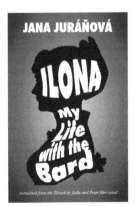

Ilona. My Life with the Bard
by Jana Juráňová
Translated by Julia
and Peter Sherwood
Fiction

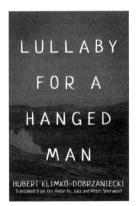

Lullaby For a Hanged Man
by Hubert Klimko-Dobrzaniecki
Translated by Julia and Peter
Sherwood
Fiction